P9-CAU-087

GOD, GRASS, AND GRACE

A THEOLOGY OF DEATH

RONALD C. STARENKO

CONCORDIA®

Publishing House
St. Louis   London

Concordia Publishing House, St. Louis, Missouri
Concordia Publishing House Ltd., London, E. C. 1
Copyright © 1975 Concordia Publishing House

MANUFACTURED IN THE UNITED STATES OF AMERICA

Library of Congress Cataloging in Publication Data

Starenko, Ronald C
        God, grass, and grace.

        Bibliography: p.
        1. Death. I. Title.
BT825.S78   236′.1   74-18244
ISBN 0-570-03198-2

CONTENTS

PREFACE

When I began the research for writing this book, I was amazed how many books had already been written about death. I was almost afraid to continue, aware of the flood of material about death already on the market and knowing that what I would attempt would not be nearly as exhaustive as many other works which I had read on the subject.

It was not my purpose, however, simply to write a book that had not been written. For a long time I have been struggling to achieve an adequate theology of death. Based on my own questions about life and death and my experience with people who were dying or grieving, I am offering here what I believe is an honest and realistic understanding of death.

I am also quite conscious of the fact that though I am a dying man like anyone else, I cannot speak as though I had died. I have, therefore, subjective feelings and hangups. What objectivity I can claim I have received through the revelation of God in Holy Scripture and through my Christian experience in the community of the church.

In defining a theology of death I have tried as consistently as possible to understand the message of Scripture and to interpret the human experience according to the Lutheran Law/Gospel principle. I believe that death is God's crushing judgment on man the sinner, symbolized by the fate of grass so often referred to in Scripture. I also believe that the death and resurrection of Jesus Christ is God's judgment on that judgment, the word of the Lord that abides forever. Thus I believe that the sinner, though he die, will live, that the forgiveness of sin by God's grace is already life in the midst of death.

It is my contention that only a Christian is able to die, to accept death as his deserved fate, and still have hope and joy. Without the good news of the Gospel I see people of necessity repressing any thought of death or romanticizing it. Quite frankly I am pessimistic about man and the world he has created. But I am not a cynic. What optimism I share about life is my hope in God. Because of His mighty and merciful deeds which He has accomplished in Jesus Christ, I am able to comfort and to celebrate with the dying.

Therefore I offer these words as yet another witness to the faith of the church which lives in the tension between a new age that has already dawned upon a dying world and that which will be fully revealed in the return of the Lord and the resurrection of all His members.

PART I

All flesh is grass, and all its beauty is like the flower of the field. The grass withers, the flower fades, when the breath of the Lord blows upon it; surely the people is grass.

(Is. 40:6b-7)

Philosophical Perspective

In his book *The Courage to Be* Paul Tillich distinguishes three types of anxiety: the anxiety about fate and death, the anxiety about guilt and condemnation, and the anxiety about emptiness and meaninglessness. By means of each he describes a period of history. The first type he finds characteristic of man until the end of the ancient civilizations, the second through the Middle Ages, and the third down to modern times. Although he is aware that such divisions cannot really be made so neatly, he has nevertheless identified the basic shifts in man's response to what threatens him. In addition to recognizing the overlapping that occurs, I would state also, as I will show later, that all forms of anxiety derive from a common fear, the fear of death. My purpose in this chapter is simply to give an overview of how man has dealt with this anxiety philosophically.

The concern of the ancients about fate led to fanaticizing heroism in the face of death. Socrates believed, for example, that death was overcome by heroically embracing it. One might say that the Greeks and Romans had a flirtation with death. As a matter of fact, Plato defined philosophy as "the preparation for death."

This is understandable, knowing their view of man as a dichotomy. If the soul, preexistent, immortal, and eternal, inhabits a body, mortal, temporary, and evil, then why shouldn't death be welcomed? Like a release from prison it is a flying home. Because the Western world has inherited and understanding of reality peculiar to the Greeks, we find this notion quite common in modern times. However, I shall discuss that at greater length in a chapter which will deal among other matters with the notion of the immortality of the soul.

That approach to death prevailed beyond the period of the ancients into the Middle Ages. And even though man's concern shifted from fate and death to guilt, the anxiety about death remained and was met with the traditional notions. The presence of guilt included the fear of punishment, and that only served to intensify man's dread of death. What was different, however, was that death was feared and not welcomed. Still, it was believed that man could win the battle against death because there was something indestructible about his nature.

With the advent of the Renaissance period and the Age of Enlightenment the philosophers assumed a new approach to death. Scientific discoveries and learning caused man to focus on his accomplishments and achievements. He was not so much concerned about dying as he was about living. Spinoza, for example, who believed that the universe was intelligently ordered, considered death to be a natural occurrence and of no consequence to a free man. It is amazing that such a notion, despite the fact that few other thinkers were as extreme in dismissing the reality of death, was largely held through the 17th, 18th, and 19th centuries. There was simply astonishingly little preoccupation in philosophy and art with human mortality, no doubt because the thought of death did not fit in with human progress, the belief in the triumph of reason, and the hope of the perfectibility of man.

In the 20th century death has been rediscovered as a philosophical idea and problem. In the thought of philosophers like Karl Jaspers and Martin Heidegger a proper understanding of death and a right attitude toward its reality enables one to gain an understanding of the world and experience authentic existence. These two men epitomize the philosophic mood of existentialism.

J. Glenn Gray defines existentialism as "a feeling of the homelessness of man." The existentialists see man compelled to live out of his element. Our natural and social environment are not a suitable home for our spirits. Thus the existentialists reject the so-called intelligibility of the universe which the romantics had swooned about, claiming that each individual must create his own meaning in life. And part of that quest is to find meaning in death as well as life. Karl Jaspers once said, "To learn to live and to learn how to die are one and the same thing."

The existentialists address themselves to the modern anxiety about emptiness and meaninglessness. Their approach to life and death differs sharply from the idealists who were so hopeful about nature and human progress and also the pessimists who assumed an attitude of hopelessness or cynical detachment. Theirs is a reaction to the attack of science upon the human spirit. The consequence of the technology of science is not the promise of the perfection of man but rather the prediction of his destruction. But modern man does not want to contemplate his destruction, because he dreads the thought of nonbeing. How to accept this nothingness is the concern of the existentialists.

In any case, death, whenever approached philosophically, is held at arm's length. It may be considered natural, inevitable, or even final, but it remains only an event to be contemplated. Philosophy has not helped man to cope with the personal and the social catastrophe that occurs when someone dies.

Contemporary Outlook

In assessing the contemporary approach to death, the ways in which we today deal with death philosophically, psychologically, and culturally, we find that finally there is nothing new in the way people of all times have met death. If man was once concerned about fate and death, then became obsessed with guilt, and in modern times dwelt upon emptiness and meaninglessness, he remained nevertheless anxious about death, and his fear of death became the fear of dying, the fear of punishment, or the fear of nothingness. The primal dread was still death. The only difference was in the ways in which people dealt with that dread.

Franz Brokenau noticed that cultures can be classified by their attitude toward death. He saw in the ancient Hellenistic world a death-accepting attitude, in Judeo-Christian culture a death-defying attitude, and in Western post-Christian culture a death-denying attitude. Today the American attitude towards death is one of denial and repression.

Death is the new obscenity. There was a time when people could not talk about the beginning of life or about sex but could discuss the end of life rather freely. Today death has become pornographic. My children, referring to my other books which missed becoming best-sellers, have urged me to write a book on sex dealing with the confessions of a profligate parson or sex in the sanctuary. A book on the pornography of death has possibilities. Surely there must be thousands of people who would eagerly buy something entitled, *Everything You Wanted to Know About Death but Were Afraid to Ask.*

Someone has already capitalized on that phenomenon. Geoffrey Gorer, the British sociologist, observes that obsession and concealment are opposite faces of the same phenomenon. Pornography and prudery can be found in the same culture. In mid-Victorian days the sins of the flesh, meaning sex, were hush-hush, and talk about death was accepted. Today the sins of the flesh, meaning death, is the unmentionable thing, while sex receives open display in magazines and movies. Whether there is a significant correlation between sex and death, I offer no hypothesis. But it seems that one of the reasons why people have become obsessed with sex and deny the existence of the afterlife is because they find death and dying too horrible to contemplate. Fearing death, they must focus on that which symbolizes life for them, and it could very well be an automobile or a can of beer.

If death cannot be faced, it must be denied. Modern man glides over the fact of death, refers to it when he must only euphemistically. One wonders how realistic is our secular culture which prides itself on its realism. Peter Berger reminds us that our culture shields us effectively from every sign of suffering and death. People go through life without seeing anyone die, let alone be born. Pain is quarantined in hospitals. Expressways permit us to travel through the blighted areas of our inner cities without noticing people in despair. Even our executions are performed with scientific efficiency. Thus, notes Berger, an American child growing up in suburbia today has an uncanny resemblance to the young Buddha, whose parents shielded him from any sight involving human suffering and death. Death, and any symbol of it, we must repress.

One of the less subtle ways of denying the reality of death is our modern funeral practices, where the corpse as a contradiction becomes a symbol of life. To dress a dead body in a gown or a tuxedo, to restore its lifelikeness cosmetically, to surround it with cut flowers, and to adore the remains with comments like, "doesn't he look healthy," or, "she's almost smiling," or, "a picture of peace," becomes a pious attempt to camouflage the reality of death.

A few years ago I attended a seminar conducted by a funeral director who presented himself to us clergymen as someone who was genuinely interested in helping people through the experience of grief. For all his professional training and experience, for all his understanding of people and their emotional needs, he was nevertheless not about to suggest that wakes be conducted with closed caskets, that memorial gifts be made to the cancer society or the heart fund or even churches rather than spending the money for flowers. He still wanted to give people what they wanted. And it was not the truth.

Viewing the corpse, it seems to me, fills but one psychological need, and that might be to convince the immediate family that their loved one is in fact dead. But surely that is not the reason for the widespread preoccupation with a dead body. It is really an attempt to tranquilize oneself about the reality of death.

The fault for this is not only to be laid at the door of funeral directors, many of whom want to provide a public service that is helpful to people. Members of the medical profession have likewise promoted a death-denying posture. Whether they refuse to acknowledge the failure of their art and skill, as represented by death, or whether they, like anyone else, also have personal problems in dealing with the reality of death, doctors in particular do not know how to help their patients cope with terminal illnesses. They are dedicated to preserving life and health even to the point of denying the possibility of death. When death appears to be inevitable or even imminent, the devices of science are still employed to provide nothing more than false hope. As a reaction to this, many hospitals across the country are conducting seminars under the supervision of qualified chaplains to help members of the medical profession deal realistically with death themselves and help others approach their own death with meaning and dignity.

The reluctance to discuss the possibility of death with a patient or even to disclose the diagnosis of a terminal disease is not something imposed by doctors alone. Family members prefer that their loved one be spared any information that might disturb. Many people believe that it is better not to know the truth, as though the purpose of life were to be as comfortable as possible regardless of the price.

And, of course, there is a price. It is simply not true that what a person doesn't know won't hurt him. While it may be true that one person can handle the data concerning his death better than another person, it is nevertheless a fact that to live with the suspicion that one might be dying is the hardest anxiety of all. When a person must throw all his energy into denying what he does not want to believe, to pretend along with others that everything is going to be OK, to refuse to come to grips with disquieting questions, he robs himself of authentic living and dying. To have to live a lie is no victory over death. It is already a yielding to it.

There are other conspirators in the attempt to mask the reality of death. They are the members of my own profession, the clergymen of the land. If it is true that the beautification of and the fascination with the corpse is death-denying, that the ritual of IVs, respirators, and brain machines is the medical way of denying death, then it is possible also for the practitioners of religion to deceive people in distress. After all, to speak about God's will without interpretation, to voice clichés about heaven, to venerate the doctrine of the immortality of the soul to

15

mourners may indeed be a ploy to escape the threat of death, may in fact be a denial of its reality. Unfortunately churches and their clergymen have not always helped people deal with reality but instead have provided death-deniers with more reasons to believe that the dead have not really died but have just passed on.

While we continue to repress the subject of death, we still have a strange fascination with it. In the August 1970 issue of *Psychology Today*, devoted to the subject of death, Edwin S. Shneidman, who has done considerable work among adolescent suicides in California, describes the death syndrome. He refers first to that group of people who have a direct or conscious role in effecting their own demise—the death-seeker, who commits suicide; the death-initiator, who takes his own life before death overtakes him; the death-ignorer, who kills himself in the belief that he will live on in another state; and the death-darer, who tries to outwit death but succumbs to it anyhow.

A second group is those who simply let death happen, like the death-welcomer, characteristic of old persons; the death-accepter, who is philosophically resigned to his fate; the death-postponer, who like most of us wants to hold off dying as long as possible; the death-disdainer, who feels he is above the whole process of dying; the death-fearer, whose phobia drives him to find omnipotence in his physical prowess or material possessions; and the death-feigner, who attempts suicide to obtain attention and sometimes ends up getting both.

The third group, categorizing those who may be characteristic of a majority of deaths, is those people who have an unconscious role in their own demise. Such people advance the date of their death by fostering the risk of their own dying, such as the death-chancer, who gambles with death; the death-hastener, whose punishing life-style leads to an early demise; the death-capitulator, whose fear of death is so great that he actually scares himself to death; and the death-experimenter, who wishes for a drugged or benumbed consciousness.

It is this latter group that intrigues me the most. This classification suggests that there is an unconscious attitude toward death at work in all of us. Sigmund Freud called this the death instinct, a primitive drive to destruction. This implies that man is a victim of unconscious drives over which he has little control or responsibility. I would contend, however, that when a person consciously seeks to repress any thought of death he thereby sets in motion unconscious feelings about what he fears. We tend to worship what we fear. William Stringfellow has more than once made the point that our culture, which fears death and represses its feelings about it, worships death. He cites our obsession with war and violence as life in the service of death.

Somehow the fear of death releases a poison into life, driving us to exploit each moment as our last, at whatever or whosoever expense. We can fool ourselves, as we often do. We can drown out the voice of death by a clatter of noises; we can run from it; we can beautify it by giving it a look big as life itself; we can invent euphemisms like "passing on" or "going home." We can worship youthfulness, vigor, health, well-being progress, success. But the cost of this cultural conspiracy of denial and avoidance is often too horrible to contemplate.

Keith Bridston makes the point that an individual or a community for whom the reality of death is not part of its value system is inviting and asking for mass phantasizing, corporate hallucination, and communal schizophrenia. He writes that death, hidden or cosmeticized, not only in funeral rites as Jessica Mitford and Evelyn Waugh have chronicled, but in the whole psyche of a society, takes terrible revenge. For example, we note that because death is denied or explained away, communities camouflage the corporate murder and killings which their systems bring about through poverty, injustice, inequality, and the other refined socioeconomic instruments of death. When death is not admitted, reality as a whole is weakened, and the goals of society become self-destructive. To repress and deny our feelings as if they were not there is to intensify these inner pressures until, like a volcano, they erupt in violent explosion. As has been said, repression does not dispose of anxiety but only forces it to assume deeper, more desperate, more destructive expression. The repression of the reality of death does not lead to the opportunity to live, which is the great delusion, but to the necessity to kill, which is the modern tragedy.

Theological Approach

Jessica Mitford wrote that looking at death is like looking at the sun, a man can look directly into it for a moment but then must turn away. Death is the great scandal in the experience of man. It is the very negation of all his experiences. Thus man has been compelled, for the sake of his existence as man, to bridge the gap by transcending death.

One way a person attempts to do this is to exercise some kind of control over his dying. Obviously one cannot choose to be born and death likewise is a limitation imposed upon all of us; still a person can reserve for himself the right to choose when and how he wishes to die. Suicide therefore becomes one way to gain mastery over death.

Another very common way to deal with death is to suppose that it is not what it seems to be, that it only appears to be final, that in reality it is overcome by our belief in an immortality created through religion or art. If we can convince ourselves that death is part of life, part of the eternal rhythm of growth and demise, then our imperishability outlasts our dying, then the individual somehow survives through his creations, through his being remembered by future generations.

This is an instance of natural theology, the assumption that death is part of life, that there is within nature itself an ability to overcome its own imperfections. It is the belief that within the evolutionary process there is a perfectibility of man. That people over centuries of time have been ground to pieces in the process does not prevent some people from imagining that there is some inherent immortality or indestructibility in the human race that will somehow transcend the boundary of death.

The Eastern notion of reincarnation is also a belief in ultimate perfectibility, that death provides each striving person with yet another opportunity to overcome his imperfections. Thus nature is good; it provides the cycle of birth, growth, and death, which should lead inevitably to a deserved immortality.

This is but another way of denying the reality of death, ascribing to it another quality. In defiance of the empirical evidence of the finiteness of his biological existence, man, almost without exception, has believed in a personal immortality. It is a belief that has assumed more the marks of a religion rather than a philosophy.

What I choose to call religious here is not synonymous with what I would define as theological. Religion, like philosophy, is essentially a creation of man, a rationalization by which man seeks to explain or authenticate his existence, the way in which he seeks to control and manipulate God. Theology, on the other hand, is based on revelation and proceeds from Biblical teaching. Without the Word of God there would be no theology. There would only be philosophical speculation or religious superstition. In this chapter, therefore, I shall try to develop a theological approach to death, stressing mainly the Law-Gospel interpretation concerning the fate of man.

I do not think we can jump into that without first disposing of the religious notion of the immortality of the soul. I am fully aware as I write this that to challenge that notion is to raise a red flag in the face of many Christians who sincerely believe that the doctrine of the immortality of the soul is part of the Biblical faith. In fact I know people who consider any questioning of that notion as a denial of the authority of the Bible or even the resurrection of Jesus Christ. I can only hope that anyone who feels like reacting at this point would retain enough open-mindedness to discover that a reexamination of the doctrine of the immortality of the soul neither threatens the authority of the Bible nor jeopardizes the Christian's affirmation of the resurrection of the body. On the contrary, if we can get beyond a belief in the immortal soul inherited from the Greeks, we will discover the fuller meaning of the Christian Gospel.

What I am questioning, therefore, is not what the Scriptures teach but what some Christians have supposed the Scriptures are teaching. The purpose of the Bible is not to foster illusions about the reality of death but to help people deal with that reality and discover in the mighty deeds of God and answer to death and an antidote to the anxiety of dying. This does not imply, however, that the Word of God eliminates by any of its affirmations the reality of death or even the reality of the anxiety we all know about death. If that were the case, then a necessary part of our experience would be excluded, namely that death is always present and our anxiety about it. Only within the context of our anxiety about death could we hear good news. If a teaching about immortality means that we do not really die, then the true condition of man is denied and the Gospel becomes a doctrine about man and not a deed performed by God. It also means that Christians would then be to blame because they have an anxiety about death which they shouldn't have, when in fact our guilt and anxiety about death are inevitable. Guilt and anxiety are part of death, and to rationalize any or all of that away is salvation by repression rather than justification, to use a Biblical term.

Paul Tillich has written that the anxiety about death is met in two ways, referring to unchristian approaches. In one way the reality of death is excluded from daily life to the highest possible degree. The dead are not allowed to show that they are dead; they are transformed into a mask of the living. The other and more important way of dealing with death is the belief in a continuation of life after death, called the immortality of the soul. This, of course, is to be distinguished from the Biblical concepts of eternal life and the resurrection of the body.

The idea of the immortality of the soul as we employ that concept today originated with the ancients and has filtered down into Christian piety via what Adolf Harnack called the "Hellenization of Christianity." It is true that New Testament terms for "soul," "body," "flesh," and "spirit" acquired a wholly new meaning in the New Testament, but Greek thought has so much influenced Western culture that our ways of perceiving reality and even understanding the New Testament are often non-Biblical.

The problem is not merely in the fact that Greek philosophy presupposes a dualism of body and soul. The New Testament also speaks of man as a dichotomy (body and soul), even as a trichotomy (body, soul, and spirit). Though all of the Scriptures conceive of man as a unit, a whole, they do acknowledge that in our persons we are physical, mental, emotional, and spiritual beings. The difficulty arises in the freight of meaning we give to body and soul. Greek dualism represented a distortion, holding that the body of man was inherently evil and subject to annihilation, while the soul of man was indestructible and capable of immortality.

It is not difficult to see that Greek dualism has influenced our cultural and religious values. It is probably enough to point out that we have not yet struggled through that outlook which sees the body and sex as something evil. Most people would classify the "sins of the flesh" as having to do with our bodiliness and earthliness, and that the good has to do with the soul.

Of course, there have always been reactions to both

sides of this view. Consciousness III, according to Charles Reich, represents the modern attempt to celebrate life here and now, to rejoice in the body, the earth, the natural. On the other hand, our culture is also experiencing a revival of the occult, supernatural psychic phenonema in opposition to the dehumanizing and depersonalizing effects of science and technology, largely the result of the Greek emphasis on objective knowledge.

In any case, Greek dualism, including the doctrine of the immortality of the soul, represents a division, a separation in the nature of man. According to this view the body and soul of man are antagonistic qualities, with the indestructible soul winning out in the end. That surely is not where the inspired authors of the New Testament locate the conflict and the tension within man.

In Pauline theology the conflict is between the two ages, the reign of sin and death, which is tied to Adam and thus to all men, and the rule of grace and new life, which is the victory of God in the death and resurrection of Jesus Christ. The tension, therefore, is between man as man under the judgment of God and man as man justified and forgiven by the grace of God. The conflict is not between a physical part of us that must die and an immortal part of us that somehow survives in the struggle. The Christian Gospel does not say that man's spirit cannot die, as though death were merely a biological necessity, but it does in fact affirm that man's entire existence, which is under the verdict of God's judgment, has been redeemed through the verdict of forgiveness accomplished in the victory of Jesus Christ. The Gospel affirms that people as sinners receive a new spirit, a new life, by the mercy of God. That is altogether different from the idea that in Jesus God saved the soul of man from its unfortunate involvement in the experience of the body and of the earth.

The word "immortality" is mentioned in four places in the New Testament, always by St. Paul. In 1 Tim. 6:16

he praises God, "who alone has immortality." In 2 Tim. 1:10 he confesses that Jesus Christ has "brought life and immortality to light through the Gospel," meaning that our Lord by virtue of His resurrection is now incorruptible and confers that new life on all His followers. In Rom. 2:7 he says that God will give eternal life "to those who by patience in well-doing seek for glory and honor and immortality." In 1 Cor. 15:51-54 Paul speaks of our mortal nature putting on immortality at the last trumpet, at the time when God will swallow up all death in the new age of the resurrection of all believers. In all these instances God alone has immortality and bestows such new life on His people.

Understandably Martin Luther believed that since God alone had immortality and life, human beings could become immortal only if He communicated His immortality to them. When Luther therefore used the word "immortality," this did not refer to the shadowy life of the soul which could not be touched by death so characteristic of traditional views. He used "immortality" as a synonym for "resurrection."

Krister Stendahl and Wolfhart Pannenberg, two prominent theologians, believe that it is useless today to speak of the immortality of the soul. In view of the unfortunate connotations that phrase has conveyed and also in view of our modern knowledge of the psychosomatic unity of man, the idea of the resurrection better expresses that the whole man, not merely his soul detached from the body, is the subject of fulfillment beyond death. It is not possible to describe the future of mankind with the teaching about the immortality of the soul. Death gets more than the outer shell of man, as suggested by the Platonic expression of the immortal soul. Indeed death reaches into the inner core of human existence and cracks all of it open. The settlement of that problem cannot be achieved simply by acknowledging that there is some immortal part of us that is untouched by decay and death. We have no hope in denying that we really die. We have no hope in simply dying. We have no hope in believing that there is a deathless element in us. Death, as someone has said, is still 100 percent. Rather, the Christian hope is expressed in the life of the resurrected Christ, who brings victory through and beyond death. We have not the hope of an endless existence but instead a new beginning. As St. Peter reminds us, "By his great mercy we have been born anew to a living hope through the resurrection of Jesus Christ from the dead." (1 Peter 1:3b)

A theology of death not only takes death with radical seriousness but takes God the same way. To say that death is biological or natural, that it is part of a great cosmic process that leads to growth and perfectibility, implies at best that death is a friend, that if we know him and accept him and submit to him we will find the truth. That is an illusion; it is an escape from the truth. It is a denial of the fact that for everyone death is a personal encounter with God, for in death God is overtaking every man.

When St. Paul declares in 1 Cor. 15:26 that death is the last enemy of man to be overthrown, he is inferring that in death God Himself is my enemy. Suggesting that, I suppose, like questioning the notion of the immortality of the soul, is not the way to become popular. It is a radical suggestion, compelling one to contemplate death in depth, to dispense with the easy solutions which claim that death is a peaceful transition to a better world or that the Somebody Up There who loves me could not possibly be angry with me.

A radical approach to death not only takes seriously that when death occurs nothing of a man escapes but also that God is putting the sinner to death. Werner Elert writes that the destructive, disrupting, depleting reign of death proceeds in accordance with God's judgment on our lives. God's law is not only a fact of life which places a limit on human existence, it is also a law of retribution upon human existence. Psalm 90 states very clearly that death is an expression of God's anger. The death of the sinner under wrath is literally a dead end for the sinner.

In 1 Cor. 15:56 St. Paul connects the presence of death to the reign of sin, and the strength of sin to the power of the Law. He writes: "The sting of death is sin, and the power of sin is the Law." Both death and the Law, God's instruments, combine to do me in. I die not because I am mortal but because I am sinful. I die because I am in a state of rebellion against God. In the Genesis account of the fall of man we learn that our first parents found death when they opted for life on their own terms. When they willed to be like gods, to be supermen, to set their own values, to establish their own worth, they separated from God. Consequently living without God becomes a dead end. At that point the Creator throws the creature back upon himself as a sign that his rebellion not only deserves the fate of death but is already the state of death.

Elsewhere Paul states that "the wages of sin is death" (Rom. 6:23). He is saying that the final payoff for the sinner is death, but in fact all along the sinner has been earning that wage. He has been fighting against his fate. In his struggle he believes that the law of God will help him remove the reproach of death, make it less scandalous, even make it less final. But what the Law drives us to do only increases our predicament. It boomerangs on us, deceiving us to believe that by our morals and values and good intentions we are earning a fate better than death. Instead we end up fighting against God by means of His law, for life under the Law only makes for greater opportunity to rebel. As Paul also wrote: "For sin, finding opportunity in the commandment, deceived me and by it killed me. . . . It was sin, working death in me through what is good, in order that sin might be shown to be sin, and through the commandment might become sinful beyond measure." (Rom. 7:11, 13b)

The Law compels us to vindicate ourselves, to find some ground on which to stand that makes us OK, that proves we are worth saving. The Law thus requires us to do the impossible. In that way the verdict of the Law—death for the sinner—hangs over us lifelong. We may curse or we may repress in our frustration, we may react with hopelessness and assume a devil-may-care attitude, or we may imagine that we will escape the judgment by building our own regimes, but the threat of death remains, a power that holds sway from the beginning of our lives.

The Law cannot quiet our fears; it can only intensify them. Helmut Thielicke writes that the terror of death consists not in its being the end or boundary in a temporal sense, but in its being the boundary for one who from the very beginning has been out of bounds. In death we see manifest the one eternal God contradicting finite man in his attempted self-elevation beyond his boundaries. Death in the Biblical sense is not the death of man the mammal but the death of man who wants to be God and who must learn that he is only man, and what is more, is also sinner.

The bondage under which every one of us lives is the fear of death. We dread it not only because everything in us cries out against the threat of extinction but also because we know that death is not the natural destiny of man, that it is God's punishment for man's sin. It is this cause-and-effect relationship between sin and death that gives death its sting. And the pressure upon us to seek life, to make life good, to overcome death seduces us into idolatry, into deeper rebellion. How can any posture under the Law succeed in defeating death? For the Law is as much our enemy as death itself, and the fear of death is not only our dread of dying, as real as that is, but is in particular our dread of God, whose verdict is upon us all our lives. Paul Tillich states that we do not fear death because we have to die but because we deserve to die. With that understanding there is no way that we can succeed in imagining that death is simply biologically part of life or that through some scheme of immortality other than the resurrection of our Lord we can still hope to escape the verdict that before God we are always failing and at last are failures.

That fear is with us always, the fear of failure. Certain diseases may be conquered or avoided, but there is never any lasting success in healing. Governments and social orders succeed for awhile, but eventually each decays and dies. We may hope for some kind of immortality in being remembered by succeeding generations, but now the threat of nuclear destruction could even doom that venture. We live in and perpetuate a world where death and failure are a condition of life, where man's attempts to hold things together are futile.

Ralph Underwager describes the sense of failure people know because the world in which they live is coming apart at the seams. Under the pressure always to succeed, the world in all its attempts relentlessly accomplishes failure. Science and technology have failed. Education too. Also democracy and communism. Reason, enlightenment, and affluence have lost out. Evolution hasn't come through. Neither has psychoanalysis, psychology, or philosophy. Instead of promises of life, for all our endeavors we have the confirmation of death. Not wanting to accept that judgment, we choose to repress rather than confess. "Never say die," "Never think death" is the opiate of the masses.

One point I have made throughout is that little is gained by repressing our awareness of death. Tranquilize the sting of death we may, but we still die; and though we have numbed ourselves concerning the fear of death, it is still the fear of death that has determined our life-style. The existentialists claim that this is by all means inauthentic existence. They encourage us instead to view death open-eyed, to achieve full exposure to the fact of our end and so fill our living with that vital experience they call truth.

I question this possibility on theological grounds. If it is true that man by repressing his awareness of death has made his living less meaningful, how does a greater consciousness and awareness of death really enhance the quality of our living? It is the dread of dying that caused the repression in the first place. How can embracing that dread enable one to conquer it? It seems to me that that courage is also an illusion. It offers the promise that if one recognizes that he lives hourly in the face of death and learns to act on that awareness, he will be able to separate the essential from the nonessential and give a more authentic quality to his life. Doesn't that really accentuate the problem? For then one is under the pressure to find always that which is essential, when death means ultimately that one has lived on that which is nonessential.

Furthermore, the existentialists unwittingly increase the sting of death by legislating what a person must do in order to make life meaningful. Their philosophy, as radical and honest as it might be, becomes still another law, another "ought" which I must fulfill and cannot. Who is aware enough of death? Who is without hangups about it? Who can understand it by his own reason or strength?

The hard tasks of self-examination and self-evaluation are simply not possible, given the hands and minds we have as tools. There is no way that we can embrace the full truth about our death and our dying without sharing the truth of God's Spirit, His word and promise of victory and new life through the mighty death and resurrection of Jesus Christ. Who can accept the verdict of death and still live except the person who has the confidence that that verdict has been reversed, that all sinners have been acquitted in one Man's death and resurrection?

No one can endure the fate of grass who has not become more than grass—the man of faith, the person who trusts a judging and forgiving God.

Some Practical Considerations

Death with Dignity

Today there is widespread reaction to the finely finished death, decorated with tubes and bottles and machines, that has become something of a production in hospitals. Many people therefore are pleading for a death that is all their own, for a death with dignity.

That is asking for a lot, not only because there seems to be a conspiracy among professional people to glorify life at the biological level and to elevate health to the top of the hierarchy of values, but also because our culture tends to deny the reality of death, which deprives people of the opportunity to approach their death as persons.

There isn't anything about human existence that is more covered over than death. For instance, the sick and the dying are conveniently confined to hospitals out of sight. Children are not permitted exposure to death. Modern funeral practices are intended to make people feel that death is not real, that the dead are really alive, rosy-cheeked and healthy looking. The same self-deception is practiced before death occurs. We live as if we will go on forever. We keep busy in life so we don't have to think about death. We strive to look young. We may not even want to be told the truth about a terminal disease, so that we might die unsuspecting. Years ago Christians prayed that God would spare them a sudden death so they would have time to prepare for their end. Today people pray that they might die swiftly, quickly, suddenly in order to escape the ordeal of death. Accordingly, doctors and family members may wish to conceal the truth from patients, anxious about death themselves and fearing that the dying person can't handle such truth. So we go through life playing games, ducking the reality of death and depriving ourselves of authentic existence.

If we will not let ourselves die, we will not be able to live. Fearing death, we will use all of our energy escaping it or covering it over. We will succumb to the idolatry of worshiping life and health. It happens in hospitals every day. Doctors are dedicated to preserving life at all costs, even to the point of keeping people alive as vegetables. Clergymen participate in the game, too, by giving false comfort, like "Everything's going to be okay"; and if a person mentions death, they respond by suggesting that he or she think about something more pleasant. Families do the same things.

People ought to know the truth about themselves; they ought to have the opportunity to decide whether they want to die hooked up to tubes or whether they wish to remain consciously aware in order to share with their family as long as possible; people ought to be able to get the affairs of their life in order, and they ought to be given a chance to make their peace with God and their fellowman.

That pushes us close to the real problem. We are reverencing death more than God. So we try to escape death in order that we can escape God, because the fear of dying is not merely the fear of the unknown or the anxiety of being mortal, but is rather the inability to reverence God, to deal with Him, to be accountable to Him. To fear anyone or anything above God is to dethrone Him. So Jesus warns us: "And do not fear those who kill the body but cannot kill the soul; rather fear Him who can destroy both soul and body in hell" (Matt. 10:28). That is God, of course.

31

He's the one who strikes us down and pins us down. Death is by His hand and into His hands.

This dimension of death has been lost in our secularized culture. We are told that death is biological or natural, that it's just part of life, or even the transition to a better life. We are encouraged to get into that rhythm of nature and accept death. But our anxiety and fear remains, because it is not a natural event. It is a personal encounter with God. Death is God's way of visiting me at the level of myself, not because I am mortal but because I am sinful. Death is the judgment that I have rebelled against God, that I have sought to put myself above Him, that I have tried every way imaginable (even denying death) to escape Him. And in death I, the sinner, am done in.

That is what we cannot face, that we are sinners who deserve to die. That is why we have to deny death, or pretend that we are good or healthy. But that is precisely why we die, because we have served death and God gives us up to it. He doesn't play games.

But who can deal with death so honestly and so fully? Who else but the person who knows and believes that death has been defeated, that the sinner has been forgiven in the death and resurrection of Jesus Christ? Death is not the final verdict or end for those who have God's promise of ultimate victory. Death remains because the sinner remains, but at last all of that will give way to newness of life, to eternal communion with God because the suffering and dying Jesus has become the living and reigning Lord. As Paul writes in 1 Cor. 15:25-28: "For He must reign until He has put all His enemies under His feet. The last enemy to be destroyed is death. 'For God has put all things in subjection under His feet.' But when it says, 'All things are put in subjection under Him,' it is plain that He is excepted who put all things under Him. When all things are subjected to Him, then the Son Himself will also be subjected to Him who put all things under Him, that God may be everything to everyone."

Now that is the new reality, that we are free from the crushing weight of God's judgment, that death, our own dying, can be faced and endured. We are beings created for fellowship with God, but even though we have chosen separation, God is able to restore us, for that is why He gathers the church together (where else do we learn how to die?), why we share the Gospel, why we celebrate the Lord's Supper, so that we may deal with death as redeemed people, that we, the dying, may share together the life of the risen Lord, that we may die as persons with dignity because we have the hope of the resurrection and the promise of life everlasting.

Grief with Hope

Grief therapy has received considerable attention of late. Clinical pastoral education has done much research into the way people react under great loss. In hospitals extensive work is being done to understand and assist persons who are dying. Granger Westberg has pioneered in this field. More recently Elizabeth Kübler-Ross, together with doctors and chaplains at the University of Chicago Hospitals and Clinics, conducted wide studies among terminal patients.

Christian congregations, where help among grief-stricken persons has traditionally occurred, have intensified their efforts to provide a healing community. The church, more than the secular professions and philosophers, has the resources to help people deal with loss. She is able to lead her people to hope in God, to recollect and celebrate the life, death, and resurrection of her Lord.

There are specific grief situations that are common to everybody, young and old. For example, in our highly mobile society one out of four families in America is changing its place of residence every year. The experience of uprootedness is sometimes destructive for children and parents. We all need close relationships, we need to know that we belong, we need stability. Frequent or sudden moves make us grieve.

Divorce is another situation that certainly creates grief in the hearts of those who lose someone once dear to them. It is almost like a living death to see the one who perhaps you still love turning his back on you, figuratively slapping you in the face. To have been jilted can cause the same kind of hurt.

There may be pain also when the day of retirement comes, whether it is arbitrary or necessary. The loss of one's productivity and usefulness is difficult to bear, and people with heavy hearts, having lost all reason for living, are in a state of grief. Surely the loss of one's job, particularly for a man in his 40s or 50s, can be a traumatic experience. It is a blow to our ability and our security. When one becomes expendable or replaceable, there is always grief.

We could mention other losses, like the absence of a child, not through death but by his going away to college or getting married. There is loss when a child turns against his parents, when a parent disinherits a child. There is grief when we lose our health, a limb, eyesight or hearing, our hands, our house, a pet. You could add others, no doubt, but these are situations of grief that compel us to face the reality of what has happened and also to move constructively in the direction of continuing our lives.

St. Paul writes that it is possible, even in the face of life's most painful loss, the death of a loved one, to pass through grief with hope. The resurrection of Jesus Christ, he says, means that there is always possibility for new life, that God can turn losses into gains, that He can help us grow through grief. He addresses Christians: "But we would not have you ignorant, brethren, concerning those who are asleep, that you may not grieve as others do who have no hope. For since we believe that Jesus died and rose again, even so, through Jesus, God will bring with Him those who have fallen asleep. . . . Therefore comfort one another with these words." (1 Thess. 4:13-14, 18)

Despite the losses we all experience, many people do not allow themselves the expression of grief. I recall hearing a conversation after a funeral. Someone said to a friend, "How did she hold up through it all?" The friend replied, "Great! She didn't even shed a tear!" That was controlled grief, and what seemed like strength or faith was only a refusal to open up. One could then almost expect some kind of collapse later.

For some reason many people believe that it is actually wrong to express grief. It's almost as though we didn't want to admit to ourselves how we feel when loss occurs or as though we were afraid to let others see how we really feel. So a mother must be strong for the sake of her children, a man cannot cry for the sake of his self-image, even a child in anger or fear may defensively hold back all feelings.

To our surprise perhaps, St. Paul says, "Grieve!" In that connection we remember the words of the psalmist, "My tears have been my food day and night" (Ps. 42:3), or the report of John that "Jesus wept" (John 11:35) at the grave of his friend Lazarus. Grieving, contrary to our culture or our taboos, can be a creative experience, an opportunity not just to express how we feel but to exercise what we believe. To grieve with hope requires faith and trust in God, but there could be no faith or trust or hope in our grieving without the knowledge of God's loving care, who promises not that we shall never have grief but that He will help us through it. And that means the possibility to become a stronger person, a deeper person, a person better able to help others who are grieving.

Elizabeth Kübler-Ross, together with a team of doctors and chaplains in Chicago, observed that people meet the fact of their dying first with denial and isolation. This is followed by anger and resentment, then depression, and finally there is acceptance and reconciliation. But that proves to be true also of people who have suffered the loss of someone else or some other kind of loss. Of course, it is not a neat process, like the seasons of the year. There is overlapping and even overleaping. Nevertheless, in successful grieving all elements are present. The unfortunate thing is that some people get bogged down in the earlier stages and never reach acceptance, adjustment, and reconciliation.

Shock or dismay is the initial reaction in the grief process. That is how we try to cushion pain. But soon one must begin to move beyond the numbness, to the emotional release. Our Western way of dealing with death, however, seems to be mostly an attempt to tranquilize our pain. The American funeral doesn't take people very far into grief; it tends rather to make people view death as unreal or encourages a kind of sentimentalizing of death. The church, too, in many instances is not very helpful, simply because it is expected to provide nothing more than a funeral ritual which only serves to reinforce what takes place in the funeral home.

Consequently people slip into the next stages — hostility toward God and others, guilt and then depression — with little help from society or church. (I suppose I should add that many people resist help at this point, too.) And then if there is no resolving of one's feelings at this level, despair frequently follows, sometimes suicide.

No doubt difficulty in the grieving process means difficulty in the life process. Although we cannot make neat distinctions, we know life is lived in stages. We think of childhood as the age of innocence, but it is something of a shock to be born and it is a painful process to come to grips with reality. One knows that especially at the time of puberty. With the discovery of self and sex and death, life becomes an encounter. That creates turbulence, and the result is often rebellion. This is the nature of adolescence, and some young people never grow out of that stage. Like a needle stuck in a groove, they go round and round playing the same reaction. Never able to rise above this level, they approach all problems with little more than resentment. When one is unable to achieve positive attitudes toward life, he is incapable of dealing with any experience of grief. Thus middle age and old age may never be affirmed.

It is hope that enables our grief to mature. Like anything else grief must grow up, where at last we experience acceptance, where we know peace with God and others, where we can adjust to the reality of loss and still move confidently into the future. It is, therefore, in time of grief that we know how important it is to believe in God and His love, how essential it is to understand His plan for us, how valuable it is to have His promises for the future. To be able to say with stubborn Job of old, "I know that my Redeemer lives" (Job 19:25) is to grieve with hope.

For that God has not only accomplished our maturity in the death and resurrection of Jesus Christ but has also sent His Holy Spirit to help us in our struggling and grieving. He has gathered us into His church, in the freedom of the Gospel, so that we can share our pain, express our anger, and nevertheless find the forgiveness of sins and the promise of life everlasting. We have a God to believe and a supporting community which He has provided to help us to suffer loss and yet not lose, to grieve — as those who have hope.

Community with Life

No doubt one of the reasons why the church today is in decline is due to a change in our culture. Technology has ushered in a new consciousness. We have become obsessed with our progress and the resulting possibilities for plenty and pleasure, all of which creates the illusion that religion is unnecessary. There is no time to devote to religious practices anyhow, and people tend to believe that religion leaves them feeling guilty about what they have and what they enjoy. So why bother?

Among our youth technology seems to have had the opposite effect, with the church losing out in another sense. Young people are revolting against a scientific and materialistic culture which is destroying the earth and depriving people of their personhood. These young people also represent a new religion, a return to nature, a revival of mysticism. To them the church is still part of the establishment, another institution oppressing the spirit of man. So why bother with it?

No doubt, in all honesty, the church has not spoken to the needs of the secularist, the humanist, and the mystic and has been turned off by the culture around it. On the other hand, in all fairness, perhaps the church has indeed given witness to the judging and redeeming grace of God in Jesus Christ and has encountered skepticism and unbelief.

In any case the church exists to gather people into a new community. She calls people to abandon their individual pursuits and give up their fragmented existence to share in the healing of the body of Christ. It is the church that is able to deal with disorder and death, to cope with reality in the power of the forgiveness of sins. The church, gathered by the Holy Spirit under the Word and the sacraments, reaches out to people in their need. With the Law she exposes need and interprets to people how they are experiencing the judgment of God. With the Gospel she meets that need and announces deliverance and new life by the grace of God. The church, through her liturgy, her ministry, her service, her fellowship, communicates to the world the life of her Lord.

Unfortunately most people think of the church and its ministry as a symbol of authority, as a means of indoctrination, as a moral guide, as an idealistic dream, or as an example of religious zeal. Each image, in its own way, represents the Law. In each case one is met with the pressure of how he ought to be, what he has to do, what he should believe. In quite a different approach St. Paul writes that God "has made us competent to be ministers of a new covenant, not in a written code but in the Spirit; for the written code kills, but the Spirit gives life." (2 Cor. 3:6)

The ministry of the church, whether that be through the preaching or teaching offices in the church or through the encouragement that all of us give to one another, is the proclaiming and sharing of the life-giving presence of the Holy Spirit. We have all been baptized in order to hold the Word of life out to one another. Anything less than that is simply to add to the burden of the Law which we carry every day.

St. Paul refers to "the written code." He is, of course, thinking of the Ten Commandments. He knew about the difficulty that people have with the Law, with rules and regulations. He knew that the law of God, instead of giving life, only kills. He understood that the trouble is not in the Law but in the lawbreaker. The Law can't make people good. How can it hope to get a good response when it confronts people as an accuser? The Law, therefore, is not a friend to man but an enemy. It can at best only define the human condition, pinpoint the precarious predicament of mankind; at worst it exposes our disharmony with God and one another and thus condemns and kills. The verdict of the Law is death.

There will always be those who have an affection for, if not a compulsion about, the Law. There are people who need symbols of authority, order above everything else. They need a code of behavior to worship and all of the rules and taboos to go with it. They need a system, something orderly that promises security. But then when they've got regimentation, they find they have no freedom; they have duty but not joy; they may even achieve a sense of accomplishment, but they don't have peace. The Law cannot satisfy.

And yet we are always being pushed to find satisfaction or to be satisfying. The written code is more than 10 commandments on paper staring us in the face. Our whole way of life is rooted in the Law. There is the Law in our home life, in society, in our workaday life. There are continuous pressures upon us, the obligations, the responsibilities we must fulfill. What is it that keeps kicking at us to keep at our jobs, to achieve and succeed, that keeps urging us to be pleasing to others? What is it that fills us with fear and guilt when we fail, that drives us with anxiety? It is the voice of the Law; it is the judgment of God against us. It is the killing effect of the written code!

And now the church should reinforce all of that as the way of life? Is that what people need? More authority, more order, more morality, more idealism, more laws, more pressure, more condemnation? The church is to be a healing community, a fellowship of people who celebrate the life which is freedom and joy in the Holy Spirit! The church lives by a covenant and not by a code!

The Spirit is not God in His judging, accusing, killing, crunching power, but the God who creates and restores, who heals and uplifts, the God who frees. Our God is the God of promise, the God who was present in the healing ministry of Jesus Christ, the God who suffered the effects of an unfulfilled code through the death of Jesus Christ, the God who fashioned out of those ashes a new covenant through the resurrected Christ, the God whose Holy Spirit is present among us in the good news of forgiveness and the offer of life.

There is a Spiritual Presence in the church that touches our lives at those points where human effort, human accomplishment, human morality cannot fulfill us. The new covenant which God has established with us in Jesus Christ reaches the emptiness and meaninglessness of our lives with the promise of new life to fill the void and conquer the dullness, gives us the courage to say "yes" to life in spite of the destructiveness around us, speaks to us the right word which unites us in love to God and to others, changes our bad, aggressive, and depressed moods into stability and serenity. The Holy Spirit can liberate us from enmity against those we love and from open revengefulness against those by whom we feel violated. The Spirit can give us strength to throw away false anxieties and to trust in the power of God's loving care. The Spirit can create warmth, give us insight, stir within us the power of prayer. The Spirit, working through the Gospel of life which we receive in the spoken Word and the Sacrament shared, can give us an experience of life that transcends law, world, and the daily grind.

We understand the need for a code. What would happen to the world without law or social pressures? Evil would go on unrestrained, and we would live in a state of confusion and disorganization. But man is a spirit with a personal need to be free, to be unafraid, to know love, to be redeemed, to be forgiven, to share hope, to have peace, to rejoice in life, to know God. For that only the covenant will do—the promise of God's presence in grace to bring confidence and sufficiency to people in need, to gather a community that lives by the vision of a new world.

PART II

The grass withers, the flower fades; but the Word of our God will stand forever.
(Is. 40:8)

The Living and the Dead

There are but two kinds of people. They are not the rich and the poor, the sinners and the saints, the pious and the profane, the religious and the irreligious. They are rather the living and the dead. The difference is not that the living are those walking about breathing oxygen, consuming food, and having fun, while the dead are those slumbering in the grave or floating about in heaven, whichever picture you wish to use.

But that is the way we usually look at things. If our blood pressure is normal and we are sexually potent and we still enjoy productive years, then we say, "That's living!" But let us discover that we have cancer, or old age is creeping up on us, or we are forced to live without a partner, or we feel like miserable failures in life, we are apt to say, "We might as well be dead." If you are lucky, you live; when your luck runs out, you die. So, as the old adage goes, "Live while you can, because you are a long time dead." The Schlitz brewers put it this way: "You only go around once in life, so grab all the gusto you can."

If that is the philosophy of life and death we have, then we are really dead. If our purpose in life is simply to find out how long we can cheat death and the grave and how much we can cram into these brief years, then we need the Easter message to give us life. When we seek life but instead find death, when we set goals only to run into dead ends, then we need a Word of life that will not disappoint us, a power that can turn the dead into the living.

In his gospel St. Luke reports that two women approached the grave of Christ, seeking the living among the dead. They represented many of the followers of Jesus who listened to His words and promises of life. They clung to the hope that He would give them something worth living for. But they didn't expect Him to die, least of all in the shame of crucifixion. And so they came to the grave nursing their wounds. They were alarmed and disturbed by His death, mourners wandering about the grave of the Lord in their helpless love, trying with pitiable means to stay the process and odor of corruption. They were seeking the Living One, but they returned to the place of the dead. And the angels rebuked them: "Why do you seek the living among the dead?" (Luke 24:5)

These women represent the modern spirit also. For example, modern funeral practices compel people to focus on the dead. In the hour of greatest need people are required to gaze at a corpse which mortuary science seeks to restore lifelike. There is no comfort in flowers, in corpses, in graves. It is seeking the living among the dead.

Take another situation, the world's desire for peace. What we depend on to keep peace between nations and assure survival on this earth is really something that brings death. The multiplying of sophisticated missiles, the use of bombs. That, too, is seeking the living among the dead.

Another example. The concern of our age has been described as "the search for ultimate meaning." In that quest we look for happiness in things. We abound in trivia and we avoid the depths. Our goal is to be well-fed, well-clad, well-coddled, and well-insured. In a world of technology and plenty, we can have whatever we want and go wherever we wish, but we have pushed ourselves to the brink of catastrophe. Mental and emotional disorders have increased in epidemic proportions. Suicide has become the

No. 2 killer among 16- to 24-year-olds. And we are depleting our natural resources to the point of crisis. We have committed the folly of seeking the living among the dead.

There are still other examples. The women turned to the grave in their grief. To what do people today turn when they suffer some significant loss, when their lives seem empty, when they are trying to forget, or even when they are trying to cope? We turn to work, to pleasure, to alcohol, to drugs. By doing so we numb our senses, destroy our potential, hasten our own death. We seek the living among the dead.

Paralleling this stupidity is a corresponding hostility toward the things of God. People no longer hear or read the Scriptures. Church attendance is in sharp decline. Many Christians are no longer disturbed that they live their lives without the Sacrament. Instead people respond only to the way and the will of their flesh, to pursuing a life-style which does not include feeding upon God's Word or participating in His Table fellowship, or identifying with His mission in the world. They are seeking the living among the dead. Any attempt to construct life without God is death.

But if those women, who came seeking the living among the dead, nevertheless heard the Word of life, then we are entitled to it today as well. The rebuke of the angels was followed by this announcement: "Remember how He told you, while He was still in Galilee, that the Son of Man must be delivered into the hands of sinful men, and be crucified, and on the third day rise" (Luke 24:6-7). The other evangelists record the following message from the mouth of the angels; "He is risen! He is not here!" To the dead comes the Word of life that Christ is alive! To people like you and me, whose sin it is that we seek life in something less than God, comes the gift of peace and forgiveness and hope. We who have tried all the ways there are to die receive again today the only way there is to live, by the saving Word and works of God!

47

He can do it for any of us, for all of us! He was capable of it in the beginning. When the creation was still unformed, God spoke and in that creative breath made order and beauty out of chaos and as it were created life out of death. And when man was nothing in and of himself, God again breathed life and we became living beings. What is more, when man fell and the creation with him, when we sought the living among the dead instead of seeking God, He rose to the occasion. In the person of His Son He exposed death for what it is, that power which deceives and enslaves people, and then crushed it by the death of Jesus. Death is not Lord; Jesus Christ is! And because the Dead One is now the Living One, because God raised Jesus from the dead, there is life for the living and the dead.

The resurrection of Jesus Christ is the difference between being the living or the dead. When we are troubled by our sins and guilt, we need not seek the living among the dead by trying to rationalize or deny or cover up our guilt. He is risen! There is mercy for us. When we are bothered by questions concerning the meaning of life, we need not run or try to escape or tranquilize ourselves into oblivion. He is risen! There is hope for the weary. When we become upset with world conditions and honestly wonder what everything will come to, we do not need to crusade for fanatical causes or bury our heads in the sand. He is risen! And there is deliverance for God's people. When we lay our dead to rest, and when we lay ourselves down to die, we need not feel that all is lost. He is risen! There is the promise of the resurrection. We do not need to seek the living among the dead, because Jesus lives and He has now become the Way, the Truth, and the Life.

Do not seek life among the dead, among the things that can only produce death! Remember that Christ died for you, that He now lives as your Lord, that He gives you new life in abundance! In Him you are not dead but alive! Alleluia!

The Interruptions of Life

What goes on in the mind of the man who arises the same time every day, takes the same road with the same people to the same destination, doing the same job, eating the same meal at the same restaurant, returning home at the same time, to be greeted by the same wife, the same children, to sleep in the same bed in order to arise and repeat the same dreary routine over and over again? To make it all worthwhile we may try to orient our life around money and success and popularity and status, not necessarily because we have decided that these are the highest values of life but because everyone else seems to be doing it. This soon becomes unconscious existence, drifting, assuming, accepting, enduring without decision; this is routine and conformity uninterrupted.

But then there are the interruptions — the failures, the disappointments — that upset our plans. There is disease, there is death, as though this world were a vast game of roulette, where somewhere along the way our number finally comes up. Such thoughts we would prefer to keep at a distance. We seem to manage much better under routine and conformity. We want our life to be our own to do with as we want. We want to be the masters of our fate. We want to live without interruptions. But that would be to live without the questions or the answers. That would not be living at all! There are interruptions in life that we might be bolted out of our unconsciousness. There is this Scripture, for instance, to interrupt us that we might live:

> Soon afterward He went to a city called Nain, and His disciples and a great crowd went with Him. As He drew near to the gate of the city, behold, a man who had died was being carried out, the only son of his mother, and she was a widow; and a large crowd from the city was with her. And when the Lord saw her, He had compassion on her and said to her, "Do not weep." And He came and touched

the bier, and the bearers stood still. And He said, "Young man, I say to you, arise." And the dead man sat up, and began to speak. And He gave him to his mother. Fear seized them all; and they glórified God, saying, "A great prophet has arisen among us!" and "God has visited His people!"   (Luke 7:11-16)

The first thing this word of God impresses on us is that the reality of life is not the routine but the interruptions, the reverses. We have here the description of a funeral procession, depicting the relentless march of men from birth to death. We see here the brokenness of life. "As He drew near to the gate of the city, behold, a man who had died was being carried out, the only son of his mother, and she was a widow." This is not an ordinary situation. St. Luke is careful about describing it as an extreme situation. If death seems to be the last thing, a premature death seems to be the last straw. Then St. Luke adds that this woman, the mother, was a widow, and that's like driving the last nail in the coffin. No picture could be more tragic — a mother loses her only son prematurely, and being also a widow is now without a name, an outcast. In those days a woman had status only through the name of a man, her husband, son, or brother. But now she had no one. Perhaps she longed to be dead also, to become unconscious.

You don't even need firsthand experiences with death or grief to begin to feel for this woman. The inescapable conclusion we would all share is that it just doesn't seem fair. She should be born for all this? Why? What had she done to deserve this? We resent such interruptions, we rebel against them. We even pretend they don't exist. But even though death is a universal reality, it remains one of the most unrecognized of facts. Few admit that they will die, and when death strikes close, they are overwhelmed, crying out, "Why did God let this happen to me?" But why not? Why should you or anybody be an exception? Death strikes without warning, the young and the old, the rich and the poor, and you are next!

That disturbs us; it interrupts our unconscious living. We must avoid it. Today we try to be blind, unconscious, deceived. The grass grows green over graves. Pain is quarantined in a hospital. The cries of the demented are swallowed up behind soundproof walls. Freeways cut through the slums so you don't see the pain. Civilization has made its primary task to deceive. "Rain, rain, go away, come again some other day." This is the age of sleep, as though we had a sign on our lives for God and others to read: DO NOT DISTURB! Think of what happens in a funeral home. The corpse is laid on a satin pillow, in the midst of mountains of flowers, with recorded music that is supposed to sooth but instead almost makes your skin crawl. All this as though everyone and everything were saying, "He is not dead," when he is so dead.

It is in this moment that we begin to ask the questions of life. Why are we here? Why does this happen? What have we done to deserve this? I say to myself, here I am, entrenched in the routine men call life, but for what? All of man's works and dreams and aspirations and achievements end in the same place—dust and ashes. When this dawns, one can no longer revolve in the endless round of child-coddling and ladder-climbing and money-grabbing and all the games of the gray-flannel world without becoming obsessed with the ultimate absurdity of it all. Only then does life thrust itself in upon us as a problem, for only then do we stand stripped of all pretenses and all civilized diversions. Like the woman in the funeral procession who had lost everything, we begin to count our losses when we have been interrupted from our sleep to behold our nothingness and nobodyness.

As Jesus meets this funeral procession, He sees this woman who symbolizes all the tragedy of the world, and we are told that "He had compassion on her." This does not mean that He felt sorry for her as though she had gotten a dirty deal in life. He doesn't say, "You don't deserve this; I will square the score." He acknowledges the verdict, for God is the One who interrupts our living. It is God who passes judgment on our presumption. It is God who is visiting us when He calls our living into question. And no one can escape that. No one can escape knowing at last— even though it be at last—that he is a poor, miserable sinner who justly deserves nothing but temporal and eternal punishment.

But then it is that one may truly begin to live, when one begins to accept the interruptions of life as God's doing, when one begins to realize that he is dealing with God. We need not pray for these interruptions. They are present everywhere in the world, anything that brings us up short— embarrassment, frustration, pain, death. We shall find that they are more than judgments; they are a call to repentance. The interruptions of life call us to trust in Him who interrupts. We are called to love a wrathful God. And how is that possible?

Because God interrupts His own wrath with love! Not only do we have in this text a picture of God's verdict on man's sin, those inevitable interruptions that puncture the bubble of life; we behold also a reversal of that judgment. Christ interrupts the interruptions. He stops the procession, quiets all the professional mourners, tells the woman not to weep, touches the bier, and speaks the word: "Young man, I say to you, arise!" And the man bolts into a sitting position and begins talking. Now, that was an unexpected interruption, an undeserved act of God's grace. The compassion of Christ does not mean that He wishes to remove from our lives what we don't really deserve, as if fate had merely played a trick on us. He wishes to remove what we *do* deserve. For that is the verdict of forgiveness. The processional of suffering and death is broken by an intervening act of God's grace, totally undeserved and unexpected. Jesus Christ is that act. The raising of the widow's son served notice that the kingdom of God had dawned, that a new age had come, that the great interruption of God among men was now occurring. The word of forgiveness and life, of promise and deliverance was being spoken and being done. It would later be spoken and done decisively in Christ's own death and resurrection. God was certainly visiting His people!

The people in the story recognized this. We are told: "Fear seized them all; and they glorified God, saying, 'A great prophet has arisen among us!' and 'God has visited His people!'" A long time had elapsed since the age of the prophets. And the Hebrew people had come to believe that the next real prophet would be the great prophet of God who would usher in the Great Day of the Lord. They had always considered a visit from that prophet, no matter what the circumstances, judgment or grace, a visit from God, a divine interruption. Now in Christ's act they experienced it, the visit of the Lord and Creator Himself, who is never at a dead end or in a blind alley, who always has room to act and to save.

The great interruption has occurred. The Messiah has come. God has visited His people. He has revealed what He ultimately wills for us. We have this witness in the proclamation of the Gospel. We are to expect nothing else. There will be no spectacular or sensational events to convince us against our will. Interruptions of all kinds will continue in life, but present among them all will stand the witness of the Gospel of forgiveness and life in Jesus Christ. All interruptions are from God. We can kick against all of them, the judgment and the grace, or we can recognize in each God's decisive but gracious way of dealing with us. In any case, the word continues to be proclaimed, the message of gracious intervention, an interruption into routine or already interrupted lives, God visiting His people. Always the word to poor sinners, to troubled and lonely souls, to those unconscious and oblivious: "Young man, I say to you, arise!"

How to Live in the End Time

The word "end" sounds so final, as though everything were about to come crashing down around our ears. Is everything lurching relentlessly to decay and death and Christians must be careful not to be caught in that cataclysmic end? What is the world coming to? Astronomers tell us that someday the earth could either freeze over or burn up. The philosophers of despair terrify us with assertions about life having no meaning, that we are going nowhere, that human living and striving is like newly hatched turtles frantically trying to reach the sea before being devoured by swooping birds of prey. And everyone lives with the unsettling thought that civilized mankind is capable of incinerating our earth with the press of a button.

Unquestionably, these fears of the end profoundly affect our behavior, the way we live. If this is all there is, this brief moment between nothing and nothing, then despair takes on the form of greed and lust. Nothing matters except our own satisfactions. All values, all meaning in life, under this umbrella of fear and dread, are determined by our pursuit of pleasure. What is there to stop a man from wanting to make a quick buck or an easy woman? If the end is approaching, what's the point of morality? And when that outlook on life begins to prevail, what is there to stop us from hastening the very end that we fear? Without sounding like a prude, I will suggest that then we will drink and smoke and indulge and work ourselves to death either by attempting to escape the end or by conceding to it.

From that standpoint St. Peter's words about the end being near may seem to offer us little encouragement. He writes:

> The end of all things is at hand; therefore keep sane and
> sober for your prayers. Above all hold unfailing your love
> for one another, since love covers a multitude of sins.
> Practice hospitality ungrudgingly to one another. As each
> has received a gift, employ it for one another, as good
> stewards of God's varied grace: whoever speaks, as one
> who utters oracles of God; whoever renders service, as one
> who renders it by the strength which God supplies; in
> order that in everything God may be glorified through
> Jesus Christ. To Him belong glory and dominion for ever
> and ever. Amen   (1 Peter 4:7-11).

If he is insinuating that the world is going down the drain,
he offers no good reason for being a Christian. If he is
voicing a threat, he certainly can't expect us to pray with
confidence and boldness, to love one another with honor
and respect, and to use our energies and abilities in a positive and constructive way. The possibility of destruction
cannot be a basis for Christian faith and life.

But contrary to what seems to be the case, the idea of
end here and elsewhere in the New Testament does not
mean *finis* but fulfillment. The idea of end here is not
that moment when everything stops but when everything
at last comes into its own. It is not the moment when God
slams the door on us and His creation but when His plan
and purposes for us in Jesus Christ unfold.

Let's try, then, to look at life now as the apostles did,
from their perspective. They had a world view that over-
comes fear, that gives a foundation to prayer and love and
stewardship. They believed, in one sense, that the end had
already arrived, that they were then living in the new age.
The resurrection of Jesus Christ signaled for them that
every destructive power at work in this world would not
and could not wrench from God His people or His creation.
For by raising Jesus God was now writing the final chapter
of history, and His finishing touches are not that He is
writing it off but that He is making it complete. So, now that

the new world has been inaugurated, the early Christians were optimistic about life. They knew that out of all the evil and disorder of these present times God would make all things new. They had their risen Lord as proof of that! They had the promised gift of the Holy Spirit as a guarantee! And so eager were they in anticipation of the fulfillment of God's plan that they believed that Christ's return was imminent, that it was about to happen in their lifetime. We have since found it necessary to revise their timetable, but not to alter their hope. The end of all things is at hand, whether that be tomorrow or 10,000 years from now. The important thing is that the new, the end, has begun, that we live now in the day and the year of our Lord.

And that means something for these days in which we live. Where this Word of God, this Word of hope and promise are lacking, there you will find impatience on the one hand and complacency on the other. The impatience of our day is present particularly among our youth. They are part of the *now* generation. Because of their passionate desire for instant achievement, be that sensual pleasure or social change, they are not inclined to wait. We must remember that they are in part the product of a technological age, of a world where we make things happen fast, and it is only natural that they should be inclined toward impatience. But a word of warning to our youth: Revolution and violence have become means in our day to effect change and get one's way. The tragedy is that revolutionists, once they achieve their goals, often become tyrants just to preserve their achievements. Furthermore, violence begets violence. A peaceful, ordered society comes about through prayer and love and creative contribution for the common good. And for that we need a view of history that sees God and His Christ bringing order out of chaos, that sees in the Gospel the promise of a new world where troubled youth have a reason to live above hopelessness and nothingness.

There is a word here, too, about adult complacency. If it is true that youth want to move too fast, adults are inclined not to want to move at all. While youth may feel that time is running out, the adult world may have yielded to the notion that time runs on and on, that things will change by and by but it's better to be satisfied (or is it bored?) with what we have and not worry about the future. And this ignores God's involvement in the life of the world, His ordering of all things and leading our lives to His gracious purposes in Christ. For where the Gospel of fulfillment energizes people, they work patiently and persistently for the good of others. There you find people offering prayer for the church and the world, showing love for one another, using manpower and money in the service of the Christ who heals us of our sin and social evil.

The end of all things is at hand! This is not a call for frenzied activity, a scare tactic. This is an urgent call of God to participate in His new age that has already dawned in the world. In one way we can say that our living now is still part of the old order where sin and death are real, where we are driven to impatience and complacency, where fear and hopelessness are brutal realities of life. But intersecting this order is something new, the age of the Christ, God's redeeming action in the Lord's death and resurrection in which we live now and by which we shall live forever. This is the Word and the life we receive by faith and share in love. This is the Word we celebrate in worship and in daily life, the Word that forgives and therefore offers the promise of fulfillment.

The church exists to announce that the end time has arrived, that it is at hand. We have been called to be God's people, to exhibit within the life of the world the signs of hope and love and peace. The church is not just a spiritual first-aid station where we put patches and splints on the victims of our fast way of life. The church is not a tourist attraction where we cater to the emotionalism and sentimentalism of religious people. The church is people in Christ hoping for something as fantastic as the resurrection, waiting for the final return of the Lord.

And so, we live in the end time. We pray, not believing that everything will turn out in this life as we want it to, but knowing that at last God will right every wrong, heal every pain, overcome every evil, and bring us out of death to life. So we pray for ourselves, for the church, for the world. We love, not with reservation, upon conditions, but fully and freely. People who have a future are able to love, but those who are trying to gobble up the moment become greedy and selfish. But living in the end time we have a new approach, a joy and a freedom that takes seriously the life which is, that loves it in God, that loves others with the recklessness and responsibility of Christ. We use our powers, contributing our minds, our motions, our money for God's purposes in church and world. Things may look bad, and they often are, but the end of all things is neither a tragedy nor a secret. We know how it will finally turn out. We have caught the vision of the Christ; we have been caught up in His new age. We walk with Him every day, giving God glory, serving one another. We are already in eternal life! Come, Lord Jesus, come!

God, Grass, and Grace

At this moment we want to forget the whole thing. We want to believe that it didn't really happen, the death of a loved one. And if we must deal with that event—and surely we must—then we want to believe that we are not forgotten. But if we give that any serious thought, we know that death and burial means just that. So far as the memory of man is concerned very few of us will even be known much less remembered by our great-grandchildren.

In several places the Bible speaks of man's fate as being like grass. In Ps. 90:5-7 Moses writes: "Thou dost sweep men away; they are like a dream, like grass which is re-newed in the morning; in the morning it flourishes and is renewed; in the evening it fades and withers. For we are consumed by Thy anger; by Thy wrath we are over-whelmed." Isaiah, quoted also by St. Peter, cries: "All flesh is grass, and all its beauty is like the flower of the field. The grass withers, the flower fades, when the breath of the Lord blows upon it; surely the people is grass" (Is. 40:6b-7). King David says pretty much the same thing: "As for man, his days are like grass; he flourishes like a flower of the field; for the wind passes over it, and it is gone, and its place knows it no more. But the steadfast love of the Lord is from everlasting to everlasting" (Ps. 103:15-17a). And St. James describes the rich man: "Like the flower of the grass he will pass away. For the sun rises with its scorching heat and withers the grass; its flower falls, and its beauty perishes. So will the rich man fade away in the midst of his pursuits." (James 1:10b-11)

That is a terrible thing to contemplate. Those words speak of extinction, a dreadful verdict of God upon our sin and presumption. Our grasslike fate implies that no matter what glory or beauty man achieves, we fade and fall in death and, in one sense, are buried and forgotten. If nothing else, this distressing fact of life drives home the truth that we cannot presume to find meaning in life in ourselves or in what we accomplish. Such a fate exposes our sin of imagining that we are gods, of living as though we were "the master of our fate and the captain of our soul." Our beauty fades not simply as a natural process but as a judg-ment on our presumption. And that is bad news!

Nevertheless words about our grasslike fate are not the last words about us. The prophet did say that "the Word of our God will stand forever." And St. Peter adds, "You have been born anew, not of perishable seed but of imperishable, through the living and abiding Word of God" (1 Peter 1:23). What we have here are more than words,

words about death or about life. The Word of God is never words about something. Holy Scripture is not about something, not lessons, slogans, instructions, or rules. The Word of God, on the one hand, is God Himself in judgment over us, condemning sin, yes, condemning the sinner. More than that, it is God in forgiveness over us, forgiving sins, yes, forgiving the sinner. The Word of God that embraces our lives is God Himself living and abiding among us.

The Word of the Lord that will stand forever is Jesus Christ. Death is God's judgment on our deeds, but Jesus Christ is God's deed of judgment upon death. The apostle Paul wrote: "For if many died through one man's trespass, much more have the grace of God and the free gift in the grace of that one man Jesus Christ abounded for many. . . . Then as one man's trespass led to condemnation for all men, so one man's act of righteousness leads to acquittal and life for all men" (Rom. 5:15, 18). In Jesus Christ God reverses our fate, the verdict of extinction no longer hanging over our heads.

From the side of our own sin, we see our fate as grass; we are nothing. Yet from the side of faith, in the light of God's grace revealed in Jesus Christ, we see ourselves as more than grass. Our Lord Himself declares as much: "But if God so clothes the grass of the field, which today is alive and tomorrow is thrown into the oven, will He not much more clothe you, O man of little faith?" (Matt. 6:30). We are more than grass, for we have been born anew and are now imperishable through the living and abiding Word of God. Christ rescues us from extinction, having suffered our fate. His cry of dereliction, "My God, My God, why hast Thou forsaken Me?" is the cry of One whose suffering encompasses the death of all men, and whose victory earns release for all men.

This Word of God—this good news being preached to you—is a message sounding forth that death and grave and burial cannot remove us from God, for He still remembers us. We have been baptized into His name, born again of imperishable seed as the very children of God. When we gather around the Table of the Lord in remembrance of Christ, God is giving us new life, remembering the death and resurrection of His own Son for us. As we lay to rest a brother, we rejoice that God remembers him, that in Jesus Christ he is imperishable.

And finally we, like grass that seems dead in winter, will come forth again to life in the resurrection of the dead, because the grace of God will stand forever.

Down but Not Out

With great suddenness a young woman has fallen. Death has cut another of us down. Fight and fume as we may, each of us, one by one, falls before what Scripture calls "the last enemy" of man. In almost pessimistic strokes the psalmist complains to God: "Thou dost sweep men away; they are like a dream." (Ps. 90:5a)

Another person has been cut down, and not only has a young woman been deprived of her life, we have been deprived of her, someone who cannot be replaced. Left behind are children without a mother, a man without a wife, not to mention the members of the family and the church that must go on without her presence and witness. The light that was once a life, a marriage, has been snuffed out.

As little as we are willing to accept it, the fact of the matter is that it is God who grinds us into the dust. We are down, not just under death, but before God. And that is the only way it can have any meaning. This woman was not taken merely by a brain hemorrhage, or whatever it was; she was cut down by God. It is God who appoints us to die, because that is the fate of the sinner. We may protest His action, but we cannot refute it. We deserve to die.

Even such a thought puts us down. The judgment that is death is inescapable. We are always facing death. We live with it even when it isn't staring us in the eye as it is now. We meet it in our handicaps, our frustrations, our puzzlement. Beneath all of the superficiality and the frivolity of our lives it is there. God is there exposing our sin, calling us into account.

But there is something different about this death we face every day. St. Paul, according to Phillips' translation, writes:

> We are handicapped on all sides, but we are never frustrated; we are puzzled, but never in despair. We are persecuted, but we never have to stand it alone: we may be knocked down but we are never knocked out! Every day we experience something of the death of the Lord Jesus, so that we may also know the power of the life of Jesus in these bodies of ours. . . . We are always facing death, but this means that you know more and more of life. Our faith is like that mentioned in the Scripture: "I believed and therefore did I speak." For we too speak because we believe, and we know for certain that He who raised the Lord Jesus from death shall also by Him raise us. We shall all stand together before Him.   (2 Cor. 4:8-14)

It is not negative talk when the apostle says that "every day we experience something of the death of the Lord Jesus." We do not die as the Lord died, under the punishing judgment of God. The cross was Christ's alone, the utter experience of being forsaken by God. That judgment is over with, suffered out of existence. What we experience of the death of the Lord Jesus is something positive. His death was a victory, God's own way of crushing Satan and the power of death. Every experience of frustration or the finality of life we know unites us with the power of the death of Christ.

We are knocked down, but we are never out for the count. St. Paul writes: "We know for certain that He who raised the Lord Jesus from death shall also by Him raise us. We shall all stand together before Him." Certainly death has spread over the whole world and we are knocked down in more ways than one, but something else has happened to change everything. Death is not the last word about us, for we live under the resurrection event. We mourn for that one among us who has fallen before death, but there is also among us One before whom death has fallen! We, dead or alive, have the living Christ. None of us ever goes down for the count, because Christ lives. And the Father who raised the Lord Jesus will raise our loved one and will make us all to stand together before Him.

There is new power in our living now. No longer is anything hopeless or meaningless. We are troubled—but never in despair. We are in struggle—but we never have to stand it alone. "We may be knocked down but we are never knocked out!" Elsewhere St. Paul expresses the same thought: "Never far from death, yet here we are alive, always 'going through it,' yet never 'going under.'" (2 Cor. 6:9). That word says something to those bent low in grief. We go through difficulty and death. We go down, but we go on. We do not live as though this were the end, for her or for ourselves. For it is right here that God picks us up to carry us in His arms, to send us on our way for new experiences, new conquests, new life, and at last the resurrection.

Kill Me or Cure Me

On occasion I have been called upon to participate in a funeral where I was acquainted with no one, living or dead. Under such circumstances it is difficult to be personal and share feelings. In this case it would be most difficult not to. For the past six months I visited our brother weekly, communed with him on several occasions. During the last weeks of his life I was at his bedside frequently. During that time there was much both of us shared of ourselves, our fears and our faith. Our brother had cancer, as you know.

Since most of our visits together were in his home, I was close to his family also. What we do together now is but a continuation of what has already begun, a mutually supportive relationship in which we bear one another's burdens. While it is true that each man must bear his own load, especially when it comes to doing his own dying, there is a mutual burden sharing, since we are all carrying the same burden of judgment. One of the things I derived from this experience is that I saw myself in my brothers. In dealing with their need I confronted my own. All of us were under the curse of death; all of us knew the judgment of God.

In reaching out to a dying brother I encountered more than sickness and death; there was also health and life in the man. There was Christ among us with His comfort and healing. When we confess our sins to one another, when we pronounce the Gospel of forgiveness upon one another, when we are cheered by the presence of the Christ who not only died for sin but was also raised again, something of health and life enters us. In the midst of the judgment of God we find His grace; in the midst of our sickness we find His health; in the midst of our sin we find His forgiveness. Indeed, all of us were under the promise of life; all of us knew the grace of God.

Yes, there was much to share. One day our brother said something I can't forget. On that occasion, almost as if he were praying, he sighed, "O God, kill me or cure me!" That may sound very much like a man who is giving up in despair. It was in fact the words of a man giving himself over to God in faith.

Once Hannah of Old Testament times, promising her son Samuel to the service of God, chanted: "The Lord kills and brings to life; He brings down to Sheol and raises up. The Lord makes poor and makes rich; He brings low, He also exalts" (1 Sam. 2:6-7). She observed what most modern people are reluctant to acknowledge, that God kills and He cures. Death is not accidental; it is providential. In one of our older funeral rubrics, not used much anymore, we recognize, for example, that "it has pleased almighty God to take . . ." In actuality we tend to believe that death comes naturally and mysteriously, though inevitably, because we do not wish to believe that our death is at the hands of God, that it is with Him that we have to do in life and death.

The presence of death, of dying persons in the world, is a sobering reminder to all of us that we are not as healthy as we think—or as good. We are not in charge of our lives; we are not in control of every situation. Our problem, of course, is not that we are not God, that we are human, but that we spend our life trying to be like God, to be our own lord and king. And God sends death to convince us that it is not and cannot be so.

It is true that a man can long for death, for relief from his misery. But it takes a great deal of courage to die into the hands of God. As a matter of fact, it is faith that believes that when we die at the hands of God we are not being wiped out to the extent that our communion with God is broken. When a man says to God, "Kill me," he is not afraid of death, because he is not afraid of God. He knows that he deserves to die, but he also believes that the God who takes his life is the living God. He trusts, because of the death of the Lord Jesus Christ who was crucified for sin under wrath and judgment, that God in His grace will deliver.

Remember, Hannah also declared: "He brings down to Sheol and raises up." God kills and God cures. It is true that in the midst of life we are dying, but it is also true that in the midst of death we are living. Suffering, pain, and death there is, but there is also forgiveness, life, and salvation. Into our miserable, sinful lives comes God and His grace. The healing of Christ is present among us in many ways — in the love and concern of friends, in the compassion of a wife, in the treatment of medicine, in the forgiveness of sins proclaimed, in the Sacrament celebrated. In the good news concerning Jesus Christ God reverses the process of judgment and death, bestows life in the resurrection. Because the Lord lives, every experience of healing now is a foretaste of the resurrection, something we can share in all our living and dying.

"God cure me!" That, too, is a profound act of faith. It takes faith to believe that our sickness, our sin, our predicament in life is so bad that only God can solve it. It takes the courage of faith to throw oneself on the mercy of God and to look to no one or nothing else for healing. Christian faith is the conviction that the One who kills me is the only One who can cure me. Christian living, therefore, from our baptism on, is the process of being killed and being cured. Ultimately it is a movement towards the resurrection through the forgiveness of sins. Finally, not even death will upset the onward working of the Holy Spirit, who will raise us in full healing at the day of our Lord Jesus Christ.

"Kill me or cure me" is faith. It is seeing in the work of God in either direction something necessary for our salvation. It is throwing oneself on the mercy of God, as our brother did, as we do now. Is it not in all of us to say to God, "Kill me or cure me," knowing that either way He will be saving us, believing that all His ways are for our good, trusting that His ways lead us back to Him? "The Lord kills and brings to life; He brings down to Sheol and raises up."

Remember Your Creator

Remember also your Creator in the days of your youth, before the evil days come and the years draw nigh when you will say, "I have no pleasure in them"; before the sun and the light and the moon and the stars are darkened and the clouds return after the rain; in the day when the keepers of the house tremble, and the strong men are bent, and the grinders cease because they are few, and those that look through the windows are dimmed, and the doors on the street are shut; when the sound of the grinding is low, and one rises up at the voice of a bird, and all the daughters of song are brought low; they are afraid also of what is high, and terrors are in the way; the almond tree blossoms, the grasshopper drags itself along, and desire fails; because man goes to his eternal home, and the mourners go about the streets; before the silver cord is snapped, or the golden bowl is broken, or the pitcher is broken at the fountain, or the wheel broken at the cistern, and the the dust returns to the earth as it was, and the spirit returns to God who gave it. Vanity of vanities, says the Preacher; all is vanity.   (Eccl. 12:1-8)

We think of a man today who lost his youth and his health and his life before his time, a man who had days in which he found no pleasure, who experienced many moments when, like a grasshopper dragging itself along, his desire often failed. Here is an example of how strong men become bent, in his case the result of multiple sclerosis. And now the silver cord has snapped, the golden bowl is broken, his dust returns to the earth, and his spirit returns to God who gave it. And when we think realistically of what can happen to people, what has happend to this man, surely all is vanity.

That is a note almost too horrible to sound. It is almost enough to send us into a tailspin of despair, to remember how this man or any man can spend his days—as we all do—dying inch by inch until we are no more. There must be something better to think about. But note that the Preacher urges us to remember not just the good days while we have them but to remember our Creator.

And that is why we have really come together today, not

simply to observe how life can waste away, but to worship the God who has the power and love to create life, to redeem it, and even resurrect it, who is able to give us hope also in this hour.

In a sense this Old Testament writer isn't too optimistic. He sees life like it is and he tells it like it is. If anything, he is terribly realistic. In the verses preceding this chapter he writes:

> For if a man lives many years, let him rejoice in them all; but let him remember that the days of darkness will be many. All that comes is vanity. Rejoice, O young man, in your youth, and let your heart cheer you in the days of your youth; walk in the ways of your heart and the sight of your eyes. But know that for all these things God will bring you into judgment. Remove vexation from your mind, and put away pain from your body; for youth and the dawn of life are vanity. (Eccl. 11:8-10)

We do not think of these things as much as we ought to. Oh yes, we think about them, but we feel we are in a race against time. We try desperately to remain young, for that is one of our gods, youthfulness. Driven as we are, whether consciously or unconsciously, to achieve something or acquire something or be something or do something, we want to beat the game. We defy the vanity of all things. And we are neither realistic nor hopeful. We are vain, remembering mainly what we want or what we don't have.

Then it is that we aren't remembering our Creator. That's why we can fall into despair. It isn't because life is fragile and futile that we lose heart, but rather because we have forgotten our Creator. Why else did God set in motion the vanity of life, except to make it quite clear to us that life will have no meaning if we live only in the dust, if we seek only our own selfish interests? It is unbelief that ruins our days, that robs us of pleasure, that makes our living empty and frustrating.

So it is not by remembering this man that we will find hope, for we are unable to remember him and rejoice that he is more than dust but is spirit as well, a child of the living God, without remembering another Man, our Lord Jesus Christ, who came upon evil days in His youth, who was bent low in death, who Himself entered into the vanity of vanities.

But that wasn't the end. The God who created us, and who loved us still despite our vanity, did not forsake His children, and finally did not forsake His only-begotten Son, but raised Him up out of vanity and restored to Him a new body and made Him to be the Lord of all, over all and in all. The Creator was still the Creator who in the beginning was able to create man out of dust and make him a living being, who was able to raise Jesus from the dust of death, who is able to turn our hearts of stone into the response of faith and obedience, who is able to raise us up on the last day.

And now because God Himself has given us this good word to remember, we are able to remember Him even at a time like this. That makes it possible for us to remember our brother, not as a man who lost his youth too soon, who died too young, who is dead and will be buried, but as one who remembered his Creator, who died realistically but not hopelessly, as one who lives with his Creator and will enjoy youth of body, mind, and soul that has no end.

The Bread of Life

The grief we know through the loss of a loved one is the most disruptive experience of life — the suffering of loneliness, fear, guilt, even hostility. In such agonizing moments we have questions and doubts, we feel pressures, we may even become sick with emptiness and bitterness. This is truly a wilderness experience.

There is, however, support in our trouble. There is

the presence of the immediate family, friends, neighbors, the church. There are memories and hopes. There is, above all, the Lord and Giver of Life to pull us up, to direct us toward constructive goals, to help us endure the dangers of the wilderness.

We have gathered today in this wilderness of grief, as we go about burying a brother, to break bread, to share the life and love of our Lord Himself for strength and hope.

On another occasion Jesus fed a hungry and weary crowd. St. John records for us Jesus' feeding of 5,000 people with the resources of two fish and five barley loaves. Afterwards, he reports, the people were ready to crown the Lord as a bread king. They saw the food more than they saw the Lord. Jesus said: "Truly, truly, I say to you, you seek Me, not because you saw signs, but because you ate your fill of the loaves. Do not labor for the food which perishes, but for the food which endures to eternal life" (John 6:26-27a). People, He observed, work themselves to death for daily bread.

What words could be more relevant for our generation? We work ourselves to death. We are driven, ever obsessed with money and success. Moving at an ulcer-producing pace, we want to find life in what our hands accomplish. We produce for our families, seeking some kind of immortality there. The day before he died our brother spoke to me about his concern for his family, his anxiety, his devotion to his work. He explained how his heart attack frustrated him. He was aware of working for the food that perishes.

Daily bread isn't enough. Even the Israelites who plodded through the desert, whom God sustained by means of heavenly manna, still dropped along the way. Jesus noted: "Your fathers ate the manna in the wilderness, and they died" (John 6:49). We know the truth of that, for a good man, a hardworking man we love, is dead.

Were it not for our brother's death, we would not be

together like this today. But how can we make this occasion the celebration of life? We live by perishable things; we live with perishable people. None of that is the Bread of Life. There is only One on whom we may feed who is Eternal Life, our Lord Jesus Christ. He said: "This is the bread which comes down from heaven. . . . If anyone eats of this bread, he will live forever; and the bread which I shall give for the life of the world is My flesh" (John 6:50-51). For a perishing world which gluts itself on things, there is a food and drink which God provides that delivers us from death, that makes us live. When Jesus gave His body broken on the cross, He was offering Himself as food for the whole world. That was His work — forgiveness, life, and salvation for all of us. And when God by His Spirit raised Him from the dead, our Lord became the Living Bread for all His people.

Aware of the power of death, in mourning for our brother, we come together to share the Bread of Life. That experience can mean several things. The sharing of the Holy Communion also means fellowship, the experience of love and acceptance. Surely we need that for our living, especially now. For another thing, it is a meal of the future, for the Christ we share is alive, and we are alive in Him and shall be resurrected by Him. In that we are united with Him, with one another, and with our brother. Jesus said: "I am the Bread of Life . . . and this is the will of Him who sent Me, that I should lose nothing of all that He has given Me, but raise it up at the last day. For this is the will of My Father, that everyone who sees the Son and believes in Him should have eternal life; and I will raise him up at the last day." (John 6:35a, 39-40)

Fifteen hours before he died our brother shared the Bread of Life with me. It was in fact a Communion with the whole congregation, because the bread and wine shared at his bedside had been consecrated and distributed in the Sunday morning celebration. He appreciated that so much, saying that it gave him hope. It was his habit, of course, to receive the Bread of Life, and that is his immortality, to be part of the Lord's body forever.

Now we go forth as members of the same body, sharing our grief and anxiety, finding forgiveness, support, and joy as we feed upon the Lord, as we love one another. There will always be a wilderness journey to make as we pass through this world, but there will always be a Living Bread to fill us and satisfy us and sustain us forever.

She Will Never See Death

Last Sunday's Gospel lesson contained these words of Jesus: "Truly, truly, I say to you, if anyone keeps My Word, he will never see death" (John 8:51). I shared them with our sister on Monday, which words turned out to be my last devotion with her. Powerful words they are, another of those incredible sayings of Jesus. In this instance He says that His words are life.

In one sense it is preposterous for Jesus to say, "If anyone keeps My Word, he will never see death." Our sister is dead. Does He mean what He says? We are puzzled. The people who first heard this saying had a similar reaction. We read: "The Jews said to Him, 'Now we know that You have a demon. Abraham died, as did the prophets; and You say, If anyone keeps My Word, he will never taste death.' Are You greater than our father Abraham, who died?" (John 8:52-53). It didn't make sense to them either.

We do see death. We see it happen to others. We see it happening to ourselves. Christian or not, every person experiences what it means to die, to be separated from others, to have one's functions cease, to enter alone the emptiness of the grave. That is the fate of us all. We see death even before we come face to face with it ourselves.

The fact of the matter is that there is more to death than what we see. If death were simply a matter of going into the grave, an experience which nothing could change, not even the words of Jesus (after all, He died too), then we would have to pretend that death doesn't really happen. Certainly not to a good person! And if we can't quite pull off that self-deception, we must conclude, along with Jesus' antagonists, that a person has got to be crazy to say or to believe that "If anyone keeps My Word, he will never see death."

Death for Jesus, however—death as described in Scripture, for that matter—was not only separation from one's own life or one's family. Death was separation from God. Death is a condition of the human race, the result of falling away from God, a no man's land without God, without meaning, without hope, and without peace, a condition that extends also over the living. Death is present before the grave appears. The grave may represent the unknown, but if it is also a sign of our sin, then it is a symbol of judgment and condemnation.

With that larger sense of death we are able to understand Jesus' words differently. He is not saying that His words will keep us out of the grave, but He does mean that they can save us from hell. Listen to other words of Jesus recorded by St. John: "Truly, truly, I say to you, he who hears My Word and believes Him who sent Me, has eternal life; he does not come into judgment, but has passed from death to life" (John 5:24). Also, "I am the Resurrection and the Life; he who believes in Me, though he die, yet shall he live, and whoever lives and believes in Me shall never die" (John 11:25-26). Jesus is declaring that His Word and promise, backed up by His works of forgiveness, by His own cross and resurrection, by His own victorious death for sinners, is life, eternal life for believers. With forgiveness and fellowship a gift, our relationship with God restored, we are alive in God, because of Jesus Christ. And we will never see death.

That was our sister's simple faith. She kept the words

of Jesus. His words were life and peace and hope for her. She never once imagined that by believing she would get out of dying. On the contrary, it was by faith that she was able to die, that she could prepare to die, that she could let go of everything—her life, her family, her dreams. Everything but Jesus' Word! For at last that was true life for her in a dying world.

We have come together today in love and respect to commemorate someone who has died, someone whom we will all miss very much. But we gather also to celebrate because our sister is very much alive. She had eternal life before she died. She was a member of the body of Christ. She lived and died by the Word of God. She knows what her Lord meant when He said, "Truly, truly, I say to you, if anyone keeps My Word, he will never see death."

Behold, I Make All Things New

This is not going to be easy, to reflect honestly and with some depth the feelings we have, and to resonate with clarity and conviction the hope we share. Like many of you I enjoyed a very close relationship with our sister. As she once stated publicly, we laughed together and cried together, when there was good news or bad news to share.

There was plenty of bad news to deal with. It started more than two years ago, when our sister first learned about the presence of the cancer which ultimately devastated her. During that time she underwent surgery seven or eight times, submitted to cobalt treatments, and toward the last endured excruciating pain. Also during that time she worked through a lot of guilt, wrestled with faith and doubt, knew anxiety about her children, and struggled to achieve a positive theology about life and death. All of that involved suffering.

To be told that one is dying is bad news. Such information is withheld from most people, usually because doctors or family members do not wish to share such news with the victim. I suppose that when it comes right down to it most of us would prefer to be deceived. We tend to believe what we want to believe. But she wanted to know, and she was so informed. She wanted to deal with death realistically and triumphantly. On one occasion she told me that it was her hope that thereby she could help people who are afraid of death or who imagine they are going to live forever.

Whether or not we find out that we have a terminal disease, the verdict on all of us is that life is terminal. The God who gives life takes it away, if not by cancer then some other way. Death is the condition of the present order of things. When your car breaks down, when cities deteriorate, when a baby cries, when a tree falls, when your body shows the effects of wear and tear, when a mother dies in the prime of life, these are signs of what the Bible calls the old order. We live in the age where man's sin and rebellion against God has been visited with the verdict of death. And that is bad news.

In this old order there is nothing that is really new. The sun that is new every morning is burning out. A new car does not stay new very long. New health does not last forever. That which we call new is still part of the old. The Bible is right when it says that there is nothing new under the sun. Everything, including us, sooner or later fades away. That is bad news. And it is sad. And that is why we know pain now. That is what every dying person feels. That is what every survivor knows. For that is what life is like in the old order.

If that is all there is to share today, the bad news, then we would be of all people the most pitiful. If bad news were the only word and experience we have, then no wonder we would want to deceive ourselves about reality, about death. If we only go around once in life, which is bad enough, no wonder we would want to grab all the gusto we can. No wonder we would want to spin illusions of grandeur and power and pleasure.

But that is the way of the hedonist, the nihilist, the atheist. It is what you would expect to find in the old order, ways of living that are filled with deception, denial, destruction. And we haven't gathered in this church today simply to acknowledge all that. We have rather come together to affirm that which is truly new, to rejoice in the God whose mercies are new every day, to hear and share the Word of God that does make all things new. We have come together to know some good news!

The Bible that I have here belonged to our sister. Remember, (parents), it was your gift to her at Christmas 1971. Inside the cover you wrote: "May you always use this word as a guide and a staff to lean on no matter what God has in store for you." Evidently there is something new in the Scriptures, some word, some promise, some event that brings in a new age. We know that God had death in store for our sister, as He has for all of us. But death is not His last word. That which is our staff to meet life in the old order is the word of His forgiveness and the promise of new life through His Son Jesus Christ. That is a word that does not grow old with the years; it cannot be tarnished or blunted; it cannot suffer the fate of the old order. As a matter of fact it is a word of defeat for the older order, for the old can no longer touch our Lord. In His mighty death and resurrection He has won a decisive victory over the powers of this world. The new has arrived. Thus St. John in his vision can quote the Lord: "Behold, I make all things new. . . . I am the Alpha and the Omega, the beginning and the end. To the thirsty I will give from the fountain of the water of life without payment. He who conquers shall have this heritage, and I will be his God and he shall be My son." (Rev. 21:5-7)

In her case, "My daughter." She believed that word, embraced that Lord. She knew the forgiveness of sins, she experienced God's grace in the midst of her fear and suffering. She had something new, something the world did not give her, something God made.

The good news of the Gospel in Jesus Christ that there is forgiveness of sins, freedom from the power of the Law, deliverance from judgment, and resurrection from death filled her with a new quality of living that was noticeable to all. As one instance, five weeks ago, as weak and sick as she was, she celebrated at this Table the new covenant which God has made with us in the body and blood of Christ. And, as another, as a gift of love to others, the cornea of her eyes have been implanted in two New York City children to help them see again. It takes a new person to do things like that.

In the midst of the old order filled with bad news the New One, our Lord Himself, is present with His new life, with good news for sinners, for sufferers, for survivors. He who sustained the faith of your sister during her trials and tests can support all of us in our grief. He has given us His victory, He has become our God forever. He gives us vision and hope. And with St. John — and with our sister too — we affirm the Good News:

> Then I saw a new heaven and a new earth; for the first heaven and the first earth had passed away, and the sea was no more. And I saw the holy city, new Jerusalem, coming down out of heaven from God, prepared as a bride adorned for her husband; and I heard a loud voice from the throne saying, "Behold, the dwelling of God is with men. He will dwell with them, and they shall be His people, and God Himself will be with them; He will wipe away every tear from their eyes, and death shall be no more, neither shall there be mourning nor crying nor pain any more, for the former things have passed away." And He who sat upon the throne said, "Behold, I make all things new." (Rev. 21:1-5)

BIBLIOGRAPHY

Benson, George. *Then Joy Breaks Through*. New York: Seabury Press, 1973.

Berger, Peter L. *The Noise of Solemn Assemblies*. Garden City: Doubleday, 1961.

Bouman, Walter R. "History and Dogma in Christology," *Concordia Theological Monthly*, XLII, 4 (April 1971), 203–221.

Braaten, Carl E. *The Future of God*. New York: Harper and Row, 1969.

Bridston, Keith. "An exercise in Poetic Theology: The Meaning of the Resurrection of Jesus Christ for Community," *Dialog*, 10, 1 (Winter 1971), 49–62.

Commission on Theology and Church Relations. *A Statement on Death, Resurrection, and Immortality*. St. Louis: Concordia Publishing House, March 15, 1969.

Cullmann, Oscar. *Christ and Time*. Philadelphia: Westminster Press, 1950.

——. *Immortality of the Soul or Resurrection of the Dead: The Witness of the New Testament*. London: The Epworth Press, 1958.

Droege, Thomas A. "The Healing Mission of the Church," *Concordia Theological Monthly*, Occasional Papers No. 2 (May 1968).

——. "A Lutheran Perspective on Human Life," *Lutheran Social Welfare*, Spring 1971 reprint.

Elert, Werner. *The Christian Ethos*, trans. Carl J. Schindler. Philadelphia: Muhlenberg Press, 1957.

Feifel, Herman. *The Meaning of Death*. New York: McGraw-Hill, 1965.

Fulton, Robert, ed. *Death and Identity*. New York: John Wiley, 1965.

Gorer, Geoffrey. *Death, Grief, and Mourning*. New York: Doubleday, 1967.

Hulme, William E. *Pastoral Care Comes of Age*. Nashville: Abingdon Press, 1970.

Johnson, Paul E. "The Faith of a Psychologist," *Pastoral Psychology*, 21, No. 207 (October 1970).

Kantonen, T. A. *Life After Death*. Philadelphia: Fortress Press, 1962.

Kübler-Ross, Elizabeth. *On Death and Dying*. New York: Macmillan, 1970.

Mitford, Jessica. *The American Way of Death*. New York: Simon and Schuster, 1963.

Moltmann, Jürgen. "The Realism of Hope: The Feast of the Resurrection and the Transformation of the Present Reality," *Concordia Theological Monthly*, XL, 3 (March 1969), 149 – 155.

Pastoral Psychology (Death and Education), 22, No. 218 (November 1971).

——. (The Theology and Psychology of Death), 23, No. 225 (June 1972).

Pelikan, Jaroslav. *Luther the Expositor* (*Luther's Works* Companion Volume). St. Louis: Concordia Publishing House, 1959.

——. *The Shape of Death*. Nashville: Abingdon Press, 1961.

Reich, Charles. *The Greening of America*. New York: Random House, 1970.

Robinson, John A. T. *On Being the Church in the World*. London: SCM Press, 1960.

——. *The Body*. London: SCM Press, 1957.

Roth, Robert P. "Man and the Meaning of Evil," *Dialog*, 3, 3 (Summer 1964), 185 – 190.

Schroeder, Edward H. "Encountering the Last Enemy," *Dialog*, 11, 3 (Summer 1972), 190 – 194.

Schwehn, Mark. "The Tenth Plague," *The Cresset*, XXXV, 5 (March 1972), 7 – 9.

Scott, Nathan A., Jr., ed. *The Modern Vision of Death*. Richmond, Va.: John Knox Press, 1967.

Schneidman, Edwin S. "The Enemy," *Psychology Today*, 4, No. 3 (August 1970).

Stendahl, Krister, ed. *Immortality and Resurrection*. New York: Macmillan, 1965.

Stringfellow, William. *Free in Obedience*. New York: Seabury Press, 1964.

——. *Instead of Death*. New York: Seabury Press, 1963.

Thielicke Helmut. *Christ and the Meaning of Life*, trans. John W. Doberstein. New York: Harper and Row, 1962.

——. *Death and Life*, trans. Edward H. Schroeder. Philadelphia: Fortress Press, 1970.

——. *How the World Began*, trans. John W. Doberstein. Philadelphia: Muhlenberg Press, 1961.

——. *I Believe*, trans. John W. Doberstein and H. George Anderson. Philadelphia: Fortress Press, 1968.

——. *The Trouble with the Church*, trans. John W. Doberstein. New York: Harper and Row, 1965.

Tillich, Paul. *The Courage to Be*. New Haven: Yale University Press, 1952.

——. *Shaking of the Foundations*. New York: Scribner's, 1950.

Underwager, Ralph C. *I Hurt Inside*. Minneapolis: Augsburg Publishing House, 1973.

Westberg, Granger. *Good Grief*. Philadelphia: Fortress Press, 1960.